NUBian Bookstore Presents

Nubian Bookstore Presents: The ABC Book Volume II

© 2020 Marcus Dewan Williams
© 2020 Nubian Bookstore

Published by
Marcus Dewan Williams
Nubian Bookstore

All rights reserved. No part of this publication may be reproduced, distributed, or transmitted in any form or by any means, including photocopying, recording, or other electronic or mechanical methods, without the prior written permission of the publisher, except in the case of brief quotations embodied in critical reviews and certain other noncommercial uses permitted by copyright law. For permission requests, write to the publisher, addressed "Attention: Permissions Coordinator," at the address below.

Nubian Bookstore
1540 Southlake Parkway
Suite 7A
Morrow, GA 30260

www.facebook.com/Nubian Bookstore

LCCN:2020916446
ISBN: 978-0-578-41681-6
Audience: 3 & Up

1. Children 2. Picture Book 3. Easy Readers
First Printing

Printed in the United States of America

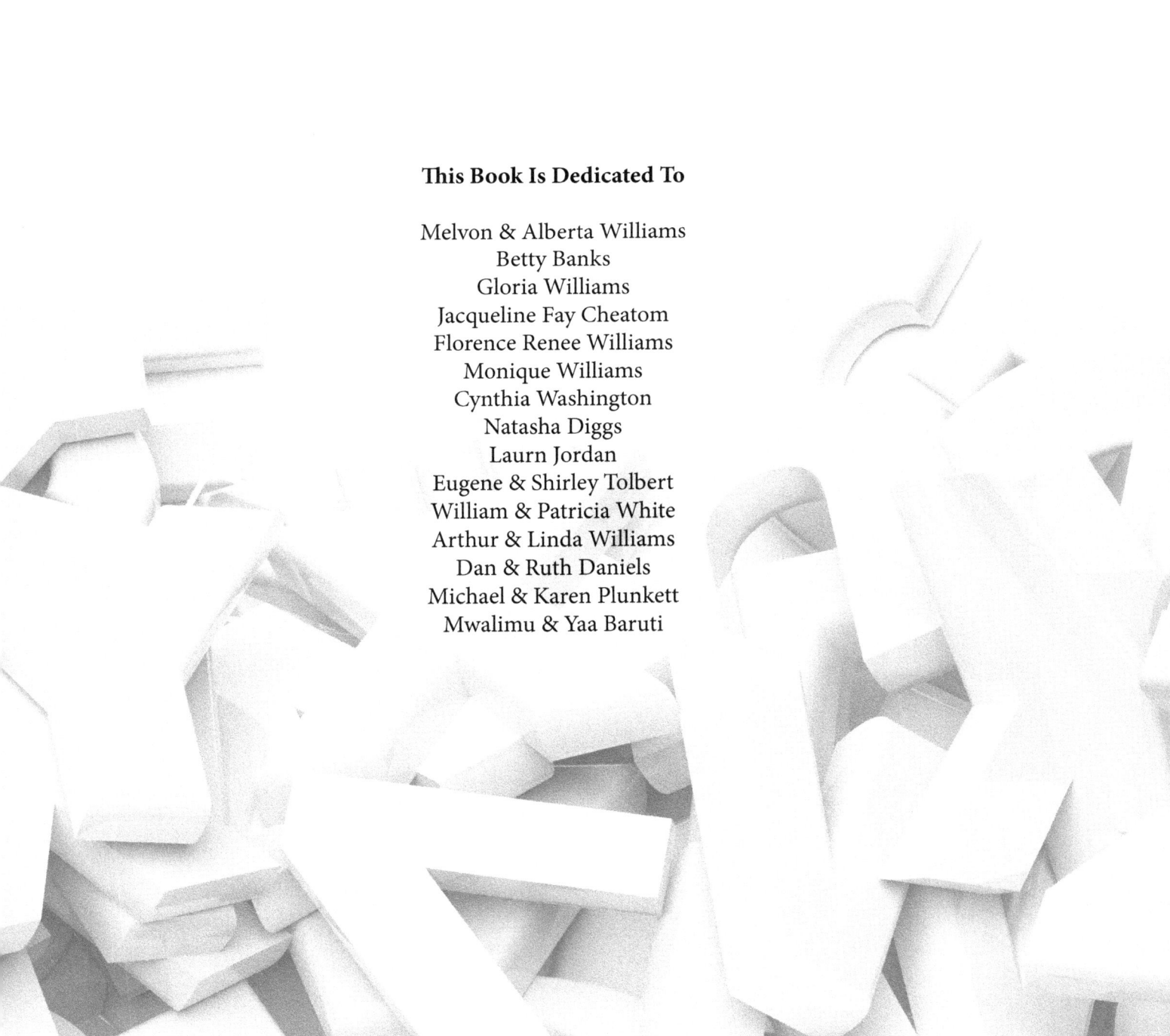

This Book Is Dedicated To

Melvon & Alberta Williams
Betty Banks
Gloria Williams
Jacqueline Fay Cheatom
Florence Renee Williams
Monique Williams
Cynthia Washington
Natasha Diggs
Laurn Jordan
Eugene & Shirley Tolbert
William & Patricia White
Arthur & Linda Williams
Dan & Ruth Daniels
Michael & Karen Plunkett
Mwalimu & Yaa Baruti

A is for Astronaut

E is for Electrician

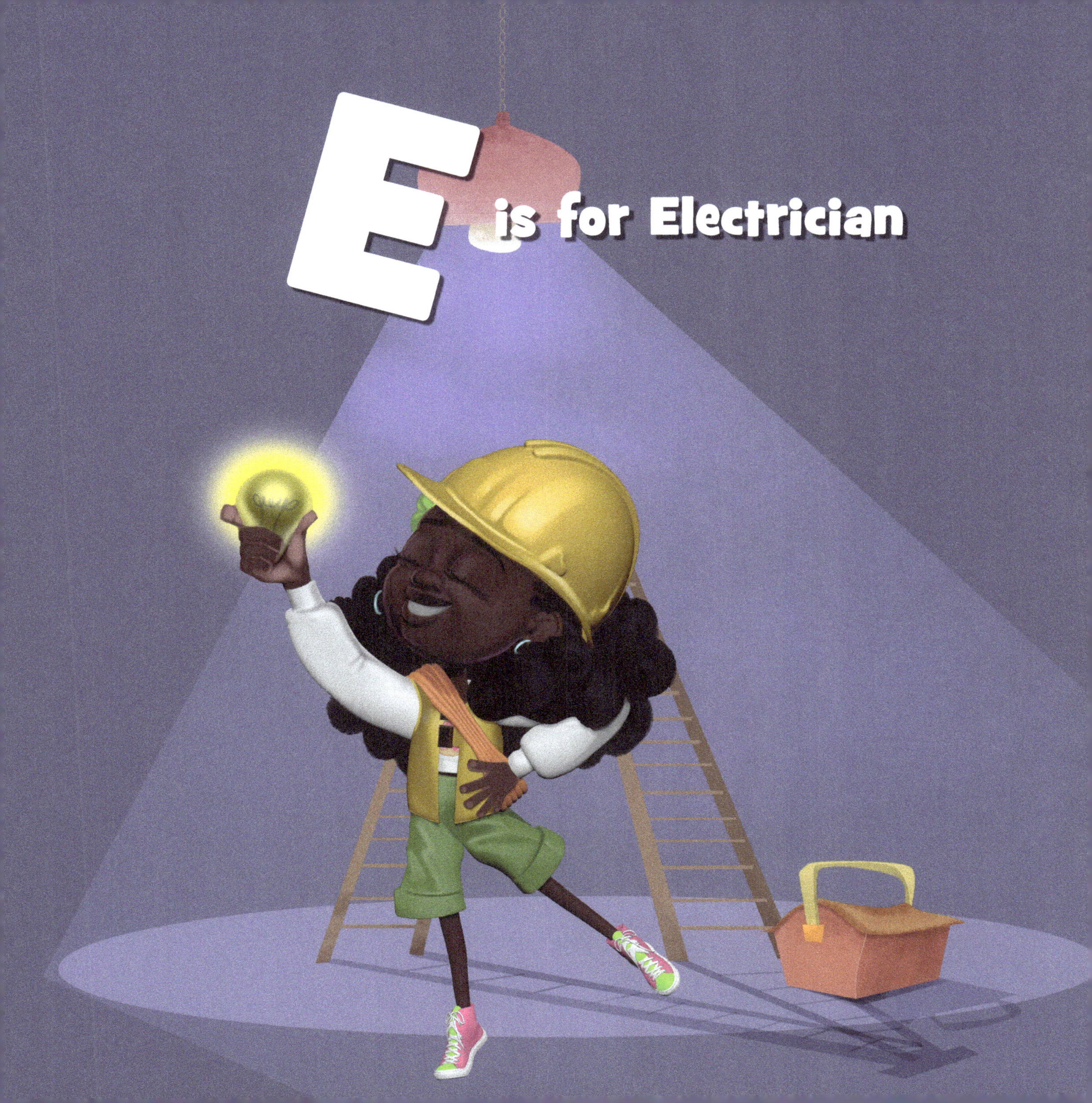

N is for Nurse

Q is for Quality Inspector

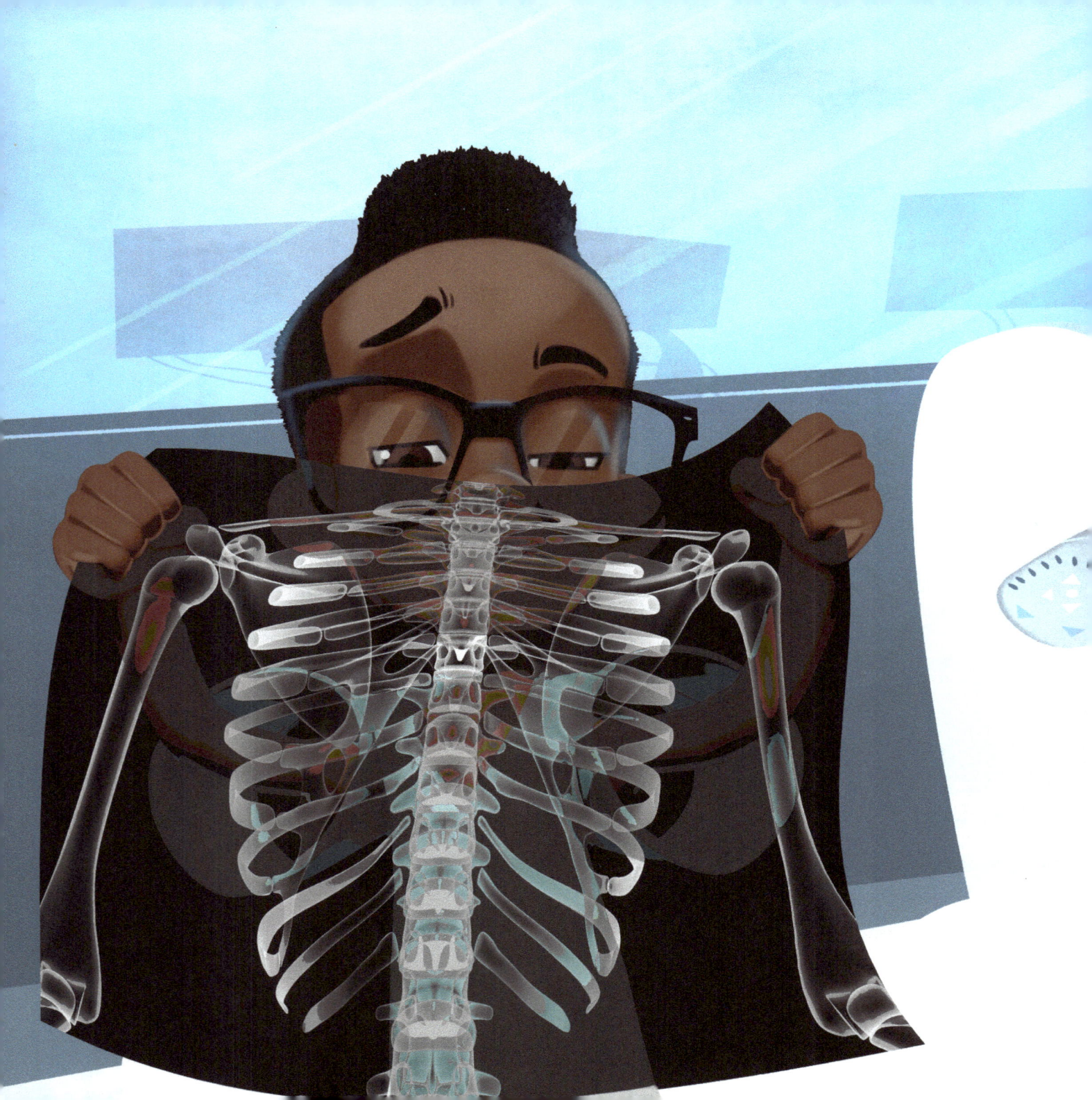

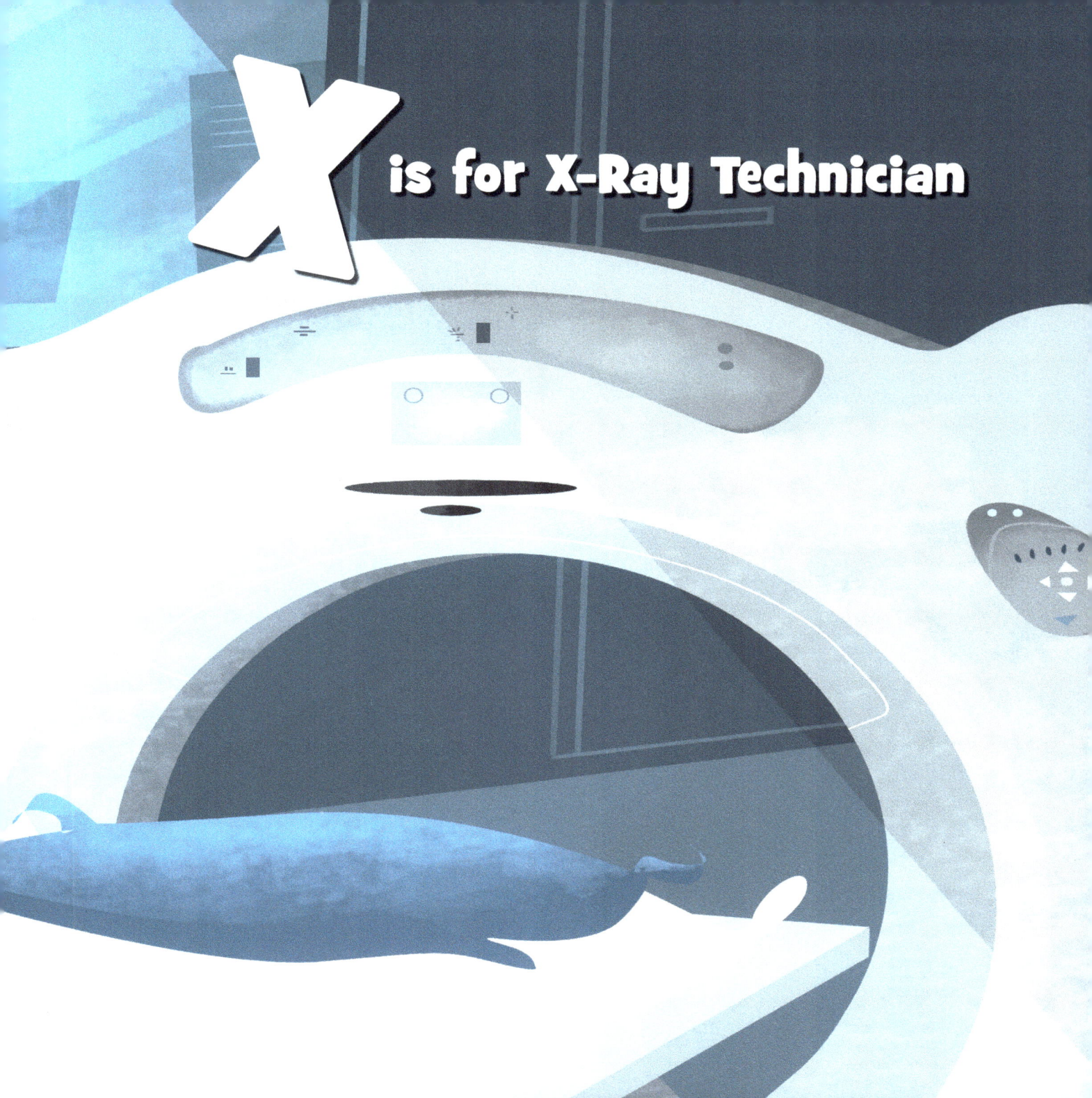

Z is for Zoo Keepers

About the Author

Marcus Williams was born and raised in Flint, Michigan. Marcus attended Morehouse College where he majored in Business Marketing, while working part-time at Medu Bookstore. His love for literature combined with his entrepreneurial drive led him to establish Nubian Bookstore in Morrow, Georgia, where he has been the proud owner for more than 21 years.

- www.facebook.com/marcusdewanwilliams
- Marcus3x@yahoo.com
- Instagram: Nubian_Bookstore

The Illustrator

Tyrus Goshay is an award-winning digital illustrator and 3D artist with over 18 years of experience. He serves as a college professor, teaching both game design, and illustration in his off time. Tyrus has a bachelor's in Computer Animation and Multimedia and a master's degree in Teaching With Technology (MALT). He has contributed to several award-winning projects in the world of Toy design and has been recognized for his achievements in academia as well. He also has tutorials in illustration and digital sculpting available on the web.
Visit his bookstore, and see other books that he has illustrated.

- www.facebook.com/Tgosketch
- Email: Tgosketch@gmail.com
- Instagram: Tgosketch
- www.tgosketch.com